Dub
Withd

/5

THE FECKIN' BOOK
of IRISH LOVE

First published 2005 as The feckin' book of Irish Sex & Love
that's not fit for dacent people's eyes by The O'Brien Press Ltd.
This edition, with new illustrations and additional material,
published 2008 by The O'Brien Press Ltd
12 Terenure Road East, Rathgar, Dublin 6, Ireland.
Tel: +353 1 4923333; Fax: +353 1 4922777
E-mail: books@obrien.ie
Website: www.obrien.ie

ISBN: 978-1-84717-099-6

British Library Cataloguing-in-Publication Data
A catalogue record for this title is available from the British Library

1 2 3 4 5 6 7 8 9 10
08 09 10 11 12
Printed by KHL, Singapore

THE FECKIN' BOOK *of* IRISH LOVE

FROM ADULTERY TO VIRGINITY AND ALL THE WOBBLY BITS IN BETWEEN

COLIN MURPHY & DONAL O'DEA

THE O'BRIEN PRESS
DUBLIN

The Feckin' Collection

Abstinence from sex

This will make you a better person. At least that's what the Church has been trying to beat into us since ancient times. The bishops really got stuck into the 'no sex please, we're Irish' thing around the seventh century, beginning with their own priests, most of whom were married. In one decree they banned sex on so many occasions (Lent, Advent, Sundays, the day the bin-man came etc) that opportunities were limited to five minutes on a Tuesday afternoon in August.

GIS A KISS!

Adultery

Adultery is, of course, a sin. And in the eyes of the Catholic church, looking at one's wife lustfully is also a form of adultery. So if you want to make love to your wife after you've had a Chinese takeaway and a bottle of red, you should go around blindfold for several hours beforehand. This may make trimming the hedge or fixing a kitchen shelf a little tricky, but at least you can enjoy your semi-drunken tumble without a mark on your soul. Although your body may look like it's been through a meat grinder.

Agony Aunts

Typical question to an Irish agony aunt in the 1960s/70s/80s: 'If a boy squeezes my breast will I become pregnant?' Typical answer: 'No, but breast-squeezing is a sin anyway, whether you're the squeezer or the squeezee. Go to confession and don't do it again.'

Among the foremost dispensers of coy advice on our love lives were the likes of Angela Macnamara and Frankie Byrne. When the phenomenon of the ultra conservative agony aunt disappeared, it solved a lot of feckin' problems.

Archbishop John Charles McQuaid

From 1940 to 1972, the Archbishop directed the course of the nation in issues of morality, and for his purposes this meant everything. This included such things as forbidding the importation of tampons as they might make women excited – *Mother of Jaysus!* Considering Dev actually got this guy to approve the 1937 Constitution before showing it to the cabinet, it's probably not surprising how sexually screwed up we were as a nation for the next half century or so. *(For issues upon which he had a direct influence see also Abstinence, Adultery, Celibacy, Censorship, Contrac ... ah, what the hell, see the entire bleedin' book!)*

Bachelor Festivals

The Ballybunion and Mullingar Bachelor Festivals offer the opportunity for eligible bachelors to make eejits of themselves in front of hordes of women, who get to holler obscenities just like men. The winner, one assumes, can expect to be ineligible for next year's competition.

In the 1970s the Ballybunion one was misleadingly called 'The Gay Bachelor Festival' – gay in those days implying jolly and carefree. The 'Gay' bit was dropped, presumably after a few of the candidates displayed a distinct lack of interest in girls.

STRANGE. THE WOMEN SEEM TO HAVE GOTTON BETTER LOOKING SINCE I ARRIVED HERE.

Bishop Eamonn Casey

(See also Celibacy, Fr Michael Cleary)

After centuries of sexual repression, the dam finally burst in 1992. And we owe it all to Eamo. Never shy to denounce the evils of pre-marital sex, it turned out that the bould bishop had had a booboo or two of his own in this regard. Literally. Luckily he was caught by the short and curlies and the rejection of the Church's teachings on sex has been snowballing ever since. For this we owe Bishop Casey a large debt of gratitude and he deserves a huge erection (of a statue) in his honour.

ERECTED
IN HONOUR
OF BISHOP
EAMONN CASEY

Book Bans

(See also Censorship, Movie Bans)

Between the 1920s and the 1950s the number of books banned rose from a handful to literally thousands. To shrieks of 'Eureka! I found a dirty word' the works of the likes of Orwell, Hemingway, Chandler, H G Wells remained off limits to Irish eyes, not to mention other parts of the body. (Well, you  have to admit, those Martians in *War of the Worlds* weren't wearing any clothes). During this sad chapter, countless books by Irish writers – James Joyce, Frank O' Connor, Edna O'Brien – also had an unhappy ending. In 1952 one member of the Censorship Board, C J O'Reilly, considered seventy books for censorship. He also banned seventy books! Ah, God be with the good oul' days.

Brehon Laws

(See also Abstinence, Celibacy, Handfasting)

The Brehon Laws are now recognised as the most advanced legal system in the ancient world. Under Brehon law, for example, women were equal partners in a marriage, of which there were ten forms. These included a marriage called the 7th degree union, which is extremely popular nowadays. It's called a one-night stand.

Celibacy

(See also Bishop Casey, Father Michael Cleary)

If we've learnt one thing about celibate priests in Ireland, it's that priests in Ireland largely aren't. And, in reality, there is no basis for them to be celibate in the first place. St Peter was married and some Popes were actually the daddies of other Popes. Similarly, in ancient Ireland farmer traditionally begat farmer, judge begat judge and priest begat priest. Until Pope Gregory VII came and screwed it up for everyone in 1079 by decreeing that all priests had to remain within the folds of the church and everything else had to remain within the folds of their cassocks. After that, misery begat misery.

Censorship

(See also Book Bans/Movie Bans)

In the Ireland of the 1930s-50s, censorship had reached such extremes that the Church/State used to employ an army of folk to cut the ads for lingerie out of foreign magazines coming into the country. The powers that be also used their muscle to trample free expression during this sad era. So to the bullies who would gladly return us to those dark days we'd like to say

3 words: Arse. Boobs.

Orgasm.

MICHELANGELO'S
DAVID
TOURS IRELAND

Churching

Up to the late 1960s, women who had given birth were required to attend the ceremony of 'churching', which involved them being blessed and 'made pure' again (service unavailable to mothers of illegitimate kids.) It was presumably the act of conceiving the child that caused the woman to be impure in the first place, which by extension, makes all of human existence a sin!

Claddagh Ring

Perhaps because it's the handiest gadget ever invented to save girls the hassle of warding off boring/ugly gougers or encouraging the attentions of hunks with loads of spondulicks, the Claddagh Ring's popularity is global. The ring features two hands holding a crowned heart with the motto 'let love and friendship reign'. Its association with the village of Claddagh in Galway? No one has a clue.

To practical matters. If you're a guy and want to check the availability of the talent/avoid a kick in the goolies, note:

On right hand, heart facing out, she's up for courtin'; on right hand, heart facing in, there's a burly boyfriend about to give you a dig in the snot locker for staring at his mot's hand; on left hand, crown out, forget it, she's hitched.

RIGHT HAND

SINGLE
(I'M LOOKING FOR LOVE)

RIGHT HAND

HAVE BOYFRIEND
(I'M FALLING IN LOVE)

LEFT HAND

MARRIED
(I WISH I'D NEVER BOUGHT
THAT DAMN RING IN THE
FIRST PLACE)

Clingfilm

Necessity is the mother of invention, and incredible as it may seem to anyone under thirty, stories abound of the lengths some would go to in order to get around the State's ban on condoms up to 1985. The manufacturers advised us to 'stretch the clingfilm securely over the object, adhering it tightly to the sides and thus preventing any spillages.' And that's exactly what a lot of people did ...

Coitus Interruptus

This is also a no-no, because 'the spilling of the seed' interferes with 'the natural consequences of sexual intercourse'. However, this being Ireland, priests pulled out from denouncing it from the pulpit, as the details were too manky/messy to go into. And of course their relative silence on the subject was taken as tacit approval (there being little alternative). Sales of tissue paper during this period went through the roof.

THAT'S NICE. FLOWERS, CHOCOLATES, A BOX OF KLEENEX?

Committee on Evil Literature

Not, as the name suggests, a group of righteous individuals doing battle with the forces of darkness, but the group which preceded the shower of savages on the Censorship Board. Sitting for only one year, 1926, their recommendations set the standards for the strict censorship of the decades ahead. Mentioned here only for their laughably dramatic title. For 'Evil' read 'Dirty'.

Condoms

These 'Sheaths of Satan' as the religious right called them, weren't truly accessible (eg in vending machines) until 1985. Between 1935 and 1979 they were banned, until Charlie Haughey's famous 'Irish solution to an Irish problem'. Within that legislation, a doctor could only prescribe condoms to over 18s, which was, ironically, two years older than the legal age for marriage! What's more, the condoms had to be for 'bona fide' family planning purposes, (i.e. couples couldn't get them if they just wanted a quick ride, though it wasn't actually expressed in those terms in the Dáil). The law was unenforceable, as the government couldn't insist on surveillance of love-making couples to keep an eye on their bona fides.

35

Confession

Traditionally, the back door through which we could escape our guilt, especially over sex. As we fell helplessly into the jaws of passion, aware of the inevitability of mortal sin, we comforted ourselves with the thought that tomorrow we would go to confession, say three Our Fathers and three Hail Marys and, Bob's yer uncle, we'd be grand with the Almighty again. So it seems God gave us guilt because he gave us sex, and confession because he gave us guilt. And in the divine plan, all three cancel each other out.

WHAT DYA MEAN YOU'RE SLEEPING WITH BIDDY O'BRIEN? I'M SLEEPING WITH BIDDY O'BRIEN?

Contraceptive Ban

It's amazing to think that up to 1935 contraceptives were actally available in Ireland. Then the government decided to outlaw their sale or import, a ban that lasted until 1979. Not content with banjaxing the country's economy for decades, people were now reminded of their incompetence at literally every conceivable moment.

Contraceptive Train

On 22 May 1971, a group from the Irish Women's Liberation Movement put the campaign for access to contraception back on track, literally. They took a train over the border into the heathen UK and bought a gansey-load of contraceptives. Back in Dublin, they expected to be arrested for illegally importing the tools of the Devil, but the authorities went limp under the media spotlight, and the women were allowed pass. Thanks to the women on the 'Durex Express', a major border had just been crossed.

Courtship Rituals

In olden days these involved such passion-killers as being chaperoned for weeks before being allowed out of parental sight and then making sure there 'was always room for the Holy Ghost' between you. Modern Irish courting rituals also severely restrict sexual activity as they involve getting completely gee-eyed, jumping into bed and then, before any funny business can happen, falling into an alcohol or drug-induced coma.

Croke Park

Believe it or not, the hallowed turf of Croker had its own small part to play in Irish love/sex lore, thanks to a story that hit the headlines in Sept 2002. Why? This was the first time someone scored at Croke Park while there was no game taking place. A courting couple, showing passion normally reserved for All Ireland Finals, scaled the gates after midnight, and by all accounts there was a lot of midfield action to follow. It's unknown how many shots they had, but they definitely had their own strip. The final result was that both midfielders were tackled by the Gardaí and sent off to court for a €500 fine. It will undoubtedly go down in GAA annals as a match that had a lot of physical contact.

ALWAYS WANTED TO GO DOWN THE TUNNEL AT CROKER...

Dance Halls

'Dens of Lust', 'Agencies of Satan', 'Vestibules of Hell' – dance halls as described by churchmen in the 1930s. In 1935 they persuaded the government to introduce the Public Dance Halls Act (co-incidentally the same year contraception was banned) which used the excuses that dance halls were 'dens of illicit drinking' to close down hundreds of dance halls. In reality the intention of the Act was to rid Ireland of an 'immoral' influence and keep women firmly in their place – the kitchen.

Divorce

In early Celtic Ireland, grounds for divorce were many and included sexual impotence due to gross obesity, telling tales about your love life, being a thief or insisting on watching bleedin' Coronation Street when there's a big match on (OK, we made that one up). Then, in 1937, divorce was banned under the Constitution, so you couldn't legally dissolve your marriage on any grounds, including wife-beating, unfaithfulness, enduring decades of mental torture etc. It's ironic that we can't actually say that the 1937 ban put us back in the Dark Ages, as in many ways the Dark Ages were much more enlightened.

Divorce Referenda

In 1986, Ireland had its first divorce referendum. Six weeks before the poll, a huge majority wanted to remove the 1937 ban. Then the Catholic right mobilised! Divorce would lead to the end of the world, a plague of locusts, a pox on all our genitals and so on ... The ban was upheld. In 1995 we got another shot and it was almost a repeat, a big lead for the 'Yes' campaign being almost reversed because of sensationalist fear tactics by a bunch of fascist gougers. And we were almost naïve enough to fall for it! The ban was lifted, but only by a tiny majority. Jaysus, what were we like?

HELLO 21ST CENTURY   BYE BYE CATHOLIC FASCISTS

Dungarvan
(Its 15 minutes of fame)

In 1995, Dungarvan (Pop 5,700), was briefly the focus of international media attention when Fr Michael Kennedy declared from the pulpit that a local woman had deliberately slept with over sixty locals to infect them with AIDS, as a revenge on men. Cue hundreds of suspicious glances from wives at husbands who were suddenly fascinated by the hymn sheet. The story spread like, well, a virus. Health experts, however, announced that the chances of a woman infecting so many men in this way were slim. Perversely, observers believed that this may have led to an increase in people throwing caution to the wind, not to mention their knickers, and indulging in casual sex, which one assumes wasn't quite Fr Kennedy's intention.

WELCOME TO
DUNGARVAN
TWINNED WITH
SODOM & GOMORRAH

Fallen Women

Not girls who have turned up in the A & E ward with cuts on their knees or twisted ankles, but those who committed the greatest of all sins – getting preggers. The problem was that it was so bleedin' visible. A pregnant single girl wandering around the village for nine months, reminding everyone that they had wobbly bits, was unthinkable. The solution was for the fallen woman's family to pack her off to a home so that the whole village could stop thinking about their thingies and return to singing songs about the Famine.

Fallen Men

As yet, historians have not found any records of this species, so it is assumed that all the fallen women were impregnated by some form of mysterious airborne sperm.

Father Michael Cleary

In the mid-1990s it emerged that another well-known cleric, Fr Michael Cleary, had fathered a child. Known as 'the singing priest', Father Cleary was out of tune with his own preaching on the evils of extra-marital sex and priestly celibacy. It hadn't really bothered most people that he'd fathered a child, just that he'd had the nerve to make such a song and dance about his flock's sinful sexual activities! And there is absolutely no truth in the rumour that his parish hymn sheet included 'Je T'aime', 'Sex Bomb' and 'Never Mind the Bollox' by the Sex Pistols.

Football Team
(giving birth to)

Nowadays, family size in Ireland conforms pretty much to the norm, i.e. 2.7465 kids. But it's a startling fact that at one point, the average number of kids in an Irish family was 10! There are a myriad of explanations for these ultra-large families: no contraception, preference for male children, marriage age very low, but the real reason is that Irish men and women are clearly the most fertile and sexually adept people on the planet.

AND KAREN, DO YOU TAKE KEITH TO HAVE AND TO HOLD AND TO BREED WITH HIM LIKE A RABBIT...

RELAX GUYS. THIS IS IRELAND. WE'LL PROBABLY ALL MAKE IT OUT OF HERE!

Gay Ireland

Up to the 1970s, the only 'Gay' living in Ireland presented 'The Late Late Show'. For most Irish people, through ignorance, innocence or denial, homosexuality did not exist. But the wider world was opening up to us in the form of travel, films, multichannel TV, literature, etc. And before we knew it, everyone had come out of the closet, in terms of awareness at least, of the gay community's existence. Homosexual acts were decriminalised in 1993, and as a measure of how far we've come since then, we've had a couple of gay lads snogging (almost) on our most popular early evening soap. Ireland's first gay/lesbian Taoiseach can't be far behind. Or maybe we've already had one?

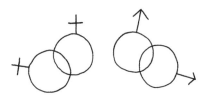

Girlie Magazines

Up to 1996, the long-suffering men of Ireland had to go to great lengths to enjoy the beauties cavorting naked in *Playboy* magazine, as girlie mags were banned. To keep abreast of the latest centrefolds, the bottom line was that you had to smuggle one in from some exotic place (like Newry or Birmingham) and risk being stigmatised for years. Nowadays you can get loads of mags with naked ladies. Or, for Mná na hÉireann, naked men. Did ye ever think we'd see the day?

Handfasting

Part of the ancient marriage ritual in which the couple getting married were literally hitched to each other with a rope around the wrists. In those enlightened days the trial marriage lasted 366 days. Then, if the wife discovered that the hubby was, say, a gargle-head with a sheep fetish, or he learned that his missus only changed her knickers once a year, they could tell each other to shag off when the period was up. This is where the term 'Tying the knot' originated. In some versions of the ritual, the knots couldn't be untied until the marriage had been consummated. Kinky, those Celts, eh?

I'LL TRY AND UNTIE THIS BIG ROPE...

AARRGGH! THAT'S NOT A ROPE!!!

In Dublin Magazine

From its launch in the 1970s, Dubliners knew that the easiest place to find sex was between the pages of this event guide. Not that it featured overt porn, but almost as titillating were the ads for Massage Parlours (brothels), the Small Ads for dirty videos and of course, its Personal Ads, some genuine, some not so. A typical one might run: 'Girl, 20s, large assets, seeks man for social intercourse. Bring money.' Who knows, maybe she really did just want to have a chat, and the money was to feed the gas meter?

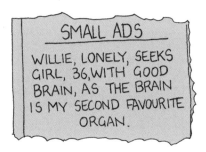

SMALL ADS

WILLIE, LONELY, SEEKS GIRL, 36, WITH GOOD BRAIN, AS THE BRAIN IS MY SECOND FAVOURITE ORGAN.

Internet

A brief search using the words 'Ireland' and 'sex' reveals that inhibition has become a dirty word. Any sexual liaison can be arranged: man/woman, man/man, woman/woman, couple/woman; you name it. Swingers used to be guys 'n' gals in flares who danced to showbands, now the only dancing Irish swingers do is the horizontal tango with someone else's wife/husband. Want sex toys, edible lingerie or a vibrating bed with mirrored ceiling delivered to Ballinamuck? No problem. And apparently a big hit with Irish couples are silk bands for tying up your partner. Must be something to do with our 800 years of bondage.

Irish Family Planning Association

Without the IFPA's tireless fight for contraceptive rights, it's probably safe to say that our largely impotent political masters would still be wondering if a spermicidal jelly would be nice with custard.

Kissing

Mothers and priests didn't discourage the widespread belief among young Irish girls that you could get pregnant through French kissing. Possibly where the word 'misconception' came from.

Lad Lane

The most appropriately named lane in Ireland, if not in the world. Lad, in case you're unaware, is a Dublin slang word for, eh, willy. And Lad Lane is the place where you're most likely to see one in action, as it is frequented by ladies of the night. It's probably just a coincidence, but it's nice to think that Dublin's 'working girls' chose Lad Lane as a place of business because they've got a really good sense of humour.

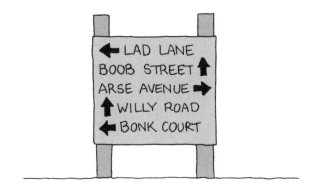

Lap Dancing Clubs

These first appeared in Dublin in the mid-1990s and have since spread to every corner of the country. For the uninitiated, a lap dance usually involves a topless/semi clothed girl dancing/hovering erotically over a man's lap, which will seem to have lost its normal flat shape and taken on a noticeably 'peaked' appearance. Most of the performers in Ireland are English girls or from Eastern Europe; Irish girls are still probably worried they'll end up dancing for their Da. In 2002, the shocked residents of the Kildare village of Milltown discovered that they had a lap dancing club in their tiny backwater. Surely not what De Valera envisioned – comely maidens lap-dancing at the crossroads?

Late Late Show, The

The Catholic, right-wing politician Oliver J Flanagan once remarked that there was no sex in Ireland before TV. More accurately, there was no sex before 'The Late Late Show'. Its host, Gay Byrne, shocked us unworldly Paddies by shooting the breeze with lesbian nuns or demonstrating the use of a condom with his finger. In an earlier show, Gay had a mock version of the 'Mr & Mrs' quiz in which he asked a contestant what she wore in bed on her honeymoon night. Her joking reply of 'nothing' brought a torrent of condemnation. How innocent we were.

Lent

In the old days, you were encouraged to abstain from many things during Lent: Meat, drinking, sweets, dancing, getting married, carnal pleasures, swearing, general merrymaking. That left knitting.

Lisdoonvarna Matchmaking Festival

Lisdoonvarna in County Clare was originally famed for the healing power of its natural spa. Nowadays, Lisdoonvarna invites you to dip your toe in the waters of romance, or any other bodily part if you get lucky. Every September thousands flock there, hoping to meet the woman/man of their dreams, as a couple of local horse-traders (literally) carry on a 200-year-old tradition of matching lonely hearts. The various stallions/fillies chew the cud over vast quantities of booze and negotiate the hurdles of getting to know one another. And if the girl gets really lucky, she'll discover she's found a stud.

WHAT DYA MEAN IT'S NOT THAT SORT OF MATCHMAKING FESTIVAL?

Lustful Thoughts

One of the Church's biggest hobby horses during Ireland's Dark Ages (1930s-1990s) was the sin of lustful thoughts. Records show that monks whose thoughts strayed inside another's underwear were rewarded with a year on bread and water. Of course, policing this relied purely on one's honesty. Imagine a woman confesses lustful thoughts to the local priest, who then has lustful thoughts about her lustful thoughts. He confesses to the canon, giving him lustful notions. He must then confess to the bishop ... the archbishop ... the cardinal. Eventually, someone has to keep their gob shut and be damned! Lustful thoughts just didn't bear thinking about.

Marriage

In Brehon times there were up to ten forms of marriage. In 20th century Ireland, marriage had only one form – insoluble. So you had better not make a pig's arse of picking your mate, because whatever happened you'd be stuck with him/her for eternity. The other thing about Irish marriage was that it was the only way legitimately to get laid. This was called the 15,000-night stand.

WHAT? YOU MEAN WE SPENT 50 GRAND ON A WEDDING AND THAT WAS IT?

HONEYMOON SUITE

Massage Parlours

In the 1980s/1990s anyone in search of a genuine massage was likely to find parts of his anatomy tended to that wouldn't be found in the Physiotherapist's Handbook. Ads featuring 'Massage Parlour' usually meant 'Brothel'. But common as this knowledge was, numerous Garda raids indicated that countless politicians, clergy and lawyers made this mistake and went seeking treatment for a particular muscle which had gone into spasm.

Masturbation

Bodily self-abuse, self-defilement or self-pollution, as it used to be called, besides being a mortal sin, produced a range of side-effects that were God's way of punishing us. Among these were blindness, stunted growth, gradual insanity, growth of hair on palms, acne, kidney infection, rectal dysfunction etc. At least that's what our short, spotty, ugly, hairy, specky, lune of a teacher told us.

NATIONAL SPERM BANK Please come ~again~

Monto

'The Monto' was Dublin's thriving red light district from 1870 until 1925. At one time, up to 1,200 ladies offered their wares in the Montgomery Street (now Foley Street) area, making it Europe's largest red light district. The Monto was frequented by many notables, including King Edward VII, presumably so he could personally acquaint his subjects with the royal sceptre.

Most Lustful
Man in Ireland

The title perhaps goes to the last High King of Ireland, Ruaidhrí Ó Conchobhair, (died in 1198, probably from exhaustion). Old Ruaidhrí is reputed to have had his wicked way with so many women that it became too much for the Pope, who had to satisfy himself with a handful. He offered to forgive Ruaidhrí if he would confine himself to having sex with just six women. Ruaidhrí's reply? 'You mean, at the same time?'

DIARY
OCTOBER
1158

MON 12	Sex
TUES 13	Sex
WED 14	Sex
THURS 15	Sex
FRI 16	Sex
SAT 17	Sex
SUN 18	Sex

Movie Bans

There have been thousands over the last century, including *Brief Encounter* (1946) for an extra-marital affair, *Ulysses,* (1967) for obscene language, *The Life of Brian,* (1979) for blasphemy, *From Dusk 'till Dawn* (1996) for violence. But for every three banned, ten 'dirty' movies were allowed through – after they'd been slashed to ribbons. See, with movies, it's easy to snip out people's naughty bits. This resulted in scenes like:

Jane: 'Frank! I want you to make me feel like a wom–'

Frank: 'I better get to work, it's almost nine.'

Jane: 'You sure you won't join me in the shower?'

Frank: 'Yes, waiter, I'll have the steak.'

Pill, The

Incredibly, given the era's anti-contraception frenzy, the Pill was available here in 1963. Had they suddenly decided to allow us let our hair down, not to mention our undies? 'Course not! Doctors could prescribe the Pill only as a cycle regulator. And good Catholic women using it thus would never stoop to taking advantage of its other side-effect: consequence-free sex. Unfortunately, if your holy Joe, bowsie, spoilsport of a doctor wouldn't prescribe the Pill, the only other legal oral contraceptive available was the word 'No.'

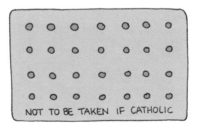

NOT TO BE TAKEN IF CATHOLIC

Polygamy

In pre-Christian Ireland, it was accepted practice for men (particularly wealthy ones) to have several wives, and though the Church opposed this when they arrived, polygamy endured for centuries. The official reason for having lots of wives was to have lots of male heirs. The unofficial reason was so that rich men could have an unlimited supply of shagging. The result was that these guys often had over thirty kids! Imagine what it was like trying to get a turn in the feckin' bathroom in the morning?

Pregnancy

When occurring out of wedlock, it was traditional to describe the pregnant cailín by one of the following quaint old Irish phrases: 'Up the pole', 'Up the flue', 'In the family way', 'A bun in the oven', 'In the pudding club', 'About to drop a chisler' or 'Up the boreen', which also supplied the probable location of where the girl had gotten up the pole. For the correct usage of these expressions, please note that they were traditionally muttered under the breath.

Rhythm Method

The only form of family planning officially endorsed by Church and State up to almost the end of the last century. But because they were too embarrassed to fully explain the technique to anyone, based as it was on the woman's menstrual cycle, lots of girls decided to interpret the title as meaning it was safe to have wild sex for about three days after a bit of fervent dancing to the local showband.

WHAT DO YOU CALL PEOPLE WHO USE THE RHYTHM METHOD?

MA AND DA?

School Dances

For many an Irish youth, this was the first contact he/she would have with the opposite sex. Actually, contact is too strong a word, as any boob/chest or groin/groin interaction would earn you a poke of a knobbly stick in the earhole from the supervising Brother or nun. For girls attending a dance, nuns reputedly wouldn't even let them wear shiny shoes in case boys could see a reflection of their knickers. Only dancing and talking was allowed. The talking inevitably got around to getting the hell out of there and finding somewhere to have a grope.

SCHOOL DANCE
TONIGHT!

NO TOUCHING,
GROPING, SNOGGING
OR LEUD TALK
ALLOWED.

MUSIC BY
ST MARYS CHOIR

COME ALONG
&
JOIN THE FUN!

Sex Education

In Ireland, education was traditionally provided by religious orders for whom sex did not officially exist – so no need for sex education. Parents stuck to 'the stork brought you' story, so sex education was confined to sniggered whispers behind the school shed. Here you had your first lesson in the biology of the opposite sex's body, the geometry of which bit went where and the mathematical impossibility of this ever happening to you. It was also where every thirteen-year-old first learned that intercourse wasn't the exam you sat in 3rd year.

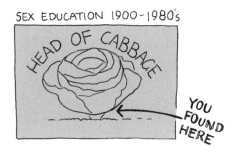

SEX EDUCATION 1900-1980's

HEAD OF CABBAGE

YOU FOUND HERE

Spike, The

Not the yoke in O'Connell Street, but a short-lived RTE TV series in the late 1970s that was as hotly debated at the time as the Keane/McCarthy affair during the World Cup. Episode 5 featured a woman posing nude for an art class. Of course, the entire country tuned in to watch. Condemnation (and axing of the series) swiftly followed, and, most famously, the founder of the League of Decency suffered a heart attack after watching the scene. Imagine how they'd have reacted to 'Sex and the City'?

St Valentine

The patron saint of mushy greeting cards ... sorry ... love, whose remains are reputed to lie in Dublin's Whitefriar Street church, a gift from Pope Gregory XVI in 1835. Before he was martyred in Rome on 14 February, AD269, Valentine miraculously cured his jailor's blind daughter and sent her a message signed 'from your Valentine'. But that's probably a load of crap. He's now a global industry, his name adorning cards, inflatable hearts, even sex toys! A million soppy or just plain rude verses

MY DARLING.
MY LOVELY WIFE.
MARRYING YOU.
BANJAXED
MY LIFE.

have been composed to mark his annual feast day. In fact, the inscription on his casket reads: Roses are awful, Violets the pits, Pull up your top, And show us your ... (Only kidding).

Terms of Endearment

Expressions of endearment *as Gailge* can be found in Irish literature stretching back millennia. Among the most popular to survive are: *A ghrá mo chroí* (Love of my heart), *Mo mhúirnín bán* (My beautiful darling), and *Póg mo thóin* (Kiss my arse). This last has the benefit that it can be used both as an expression of anger and of affection.

Unfortunate Girls

The term given to prostitutes in the early part of the last century. In those days many girls arrived in the capital from impoverished rural homes in search of work, often to be abused by their greedy, gouger employers, and then turning to prostitution in desperation. Today, of course, that's all changed. Now the girls come from impoverished countries in Eastern Europe to be abused by their greedy gouger employers.

LOOK MA! I MADE A FORTUNE BEING UNFORTUNATE LAST NIGHT.

Viagra

Given Ireland's sexual history, it's paradoxical that the small town of Ringaskiddy in Cork should be the place that, since the mid 1990s, has been giving a lift to people's sex lives all over the world. Since US drug giant Pfizer erected their Viagra plant, the area's previously limp economy has grown enormously and earned it the nickname Viagra Falls. The local name for the drug is 'De Pfizer Riser' and rumours have abounded of a baby boom in the area due to emissions from the plant, but the hard facts refute this. Aside from that, it seems that unless sex suddenly becomes unpopular, the town's fortunes will continue to rise and rise.

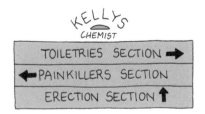

Virginity

One of the traditional Irish ways to scare girls into retaining their virginity was for a nun to pull the petals off a flower, then ask one of the class to come up and replace them. Impossible, of course, and it was equally impossible to get your virginity back. And what man would want a flower with no petals? This practice gave the English language the term 'to deflower'. It also gave us a huge number of really pissed-off gardeners.

REMEMBER GIRLS. ONE LITTLE PRICK AND IT'S GONE FOREVER.

COLIN MURPHY is the co-author of the Feckin' series of books on different aspects of Irish culture, including such diverse subjects as the Irish Character, Irish Slang, Irish Songs and Irish Sayings. He has also devoted much of his career to studying the subject of sex. Unfortunately his career has nothing to do with sex, so he's been fired 12 times. His first attempt to pick up a girl at the age of 15 resulted in him putting his back out, as he'd taken the phrase 'pick up' literally. He is also fascinated with the study of sex in the middle ages, particularly as he's in his forties himself. When he is not writing these books, he is the Joint Creative Director of one of Ireland's leading advertising agencies, Owens DDB. He is married with two teenagers who are so expensive, the royalties from this book will barely pay for a week's downloads from iTunes.

DONAL O'DEA is also the co-author of the Feckin' series. He brought a particular level of insight into the Irish Insults book as he himself has been called everything under the sun. He also considers himself an expert on matters of sex, being a frequent viewer of The Lingerie Channel and hundreds of women would love to get their hands on him, as he owes them a lot of money. Now in his early forties, he had his first real experience of sex like many others, behind the bike shed, and that was just three years ago. He spent an entire year researching this book, then his subscription to Playboy expired. He too is the Joint Creative Director of Owens DDB where he was once actually spotted doing some work. He is married with three noisy children and manages the local kids' football team who have just been relegated to the newly formed 27th Division.

What are we feckin' like?

THE BOOK *of* IRISH CHARACTERS

Celebrity Criminal

The key to star status in the Irish criminal underworld is not ruthlessness or cunning or leadership, it's finding a catchy nickname that the tabloids can have some wordplay with. For example, 'The General Outflanks the Gardaí again'. Your nickname can reflect your animal instincts (The Viper), or your perceived lifestyle (The Monk), but it should always be colourful and snappy. Rumour has it that among the hopefuls who didn't quite make it to the criminal fraternity were those who chose the following nicknames: The Undercover Guard, The Big-Mouthed Gobshite and the Lesser-Spotted Tit Warbler.

GARDAI ARREST WRONG MONK. MONASTERY OUTRAGED.

GAA Diehard

This head-the-ball will blather you into your grave with arguments about how Gaelic football and hurling are much tougher sports than soccer or rugby. He can name every All-Ireland winner since the shaggin' dinosaurs walked the earth and he has been to every GAA ground in the country in all weathers, thereby proving that not only is he committed, but also that he should be.

He is most likely a republican with a dislike of Brits and will bore the arse off you about the disgrace of the hallowed ground of Croker being opened to these 'foreign' games. He is also likely to be the gobshite spotted at the Ireland-England rugby match holding up a 'No Foreign Games' sign while wearing a Celtic shirt.

Get the rest of the
Feckin' Collection

www.obrien.ie